Plotting to Treasure

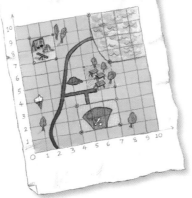

by Katherine Lindsey
illustrated by John Bendall-Brunello

HOUGHTON MIFFLIN   BOSTON

Printed in China

ISBN 10: 0-618-89899-9
ISBN 13: 978-0-618-89899-2

10 11 12 13 0940   16 15 14 13
4500432010

"Here, puppy! Come here, girl!" Ana called frantically. She stopped and whistled loudly. Then she cocked her head to listen, but she didn't hear anything—not a bark nor a whimper.

Ana spotted Manuel and Leon farther down the sidewalk. They were looking at a piece of paper.

Ana hurried toward them. "Have either of you seen a golden retriever puppy?" she asked. "I just got her two days ago. I haven't even named her yet. I thought her collar was buckled snugly, but she slipped out of it during our walk."

Manuel shook his head and said, "No, we haven't seen a puppy, but let's ask Grace. She's in the park right now."

Manuel held a walkie-talkie up to his mouth. "Grace, have you seen a puppy running around?"

Immediately the receiver began to crackle. "Was it a little golden-colored dog?" a voice asked. "If so, I saw it at point (1,2)."

"That's got to be my puppy!" Ana exclaimed. "But what point is Grace talking about?"

Leon showed Ana the paper he was holding. It looked like a map of the park, but it was covered with lines running side to side and up and down. "We're playing a treasure hunt game," he said. "One of us hides something and gives clues about it. The other two use this graph to find the treasure."

Read·Think·Write What is a point on a graph?

"We drew a map of the park and added a coordinate grid over it," Manuel explained. "The numbered line along the bottom is the horizontal axis, or x-axis. The numbered line that goes up is the vertical axis, or y-axis. A number from the x-axis followed by a number from the y-axis is an ordered pair. The ordered pairs are the clues that direct us to the treasure."

Ana was still confused.

"What Manuel means is that we take the first number in the ordered pair and move that many units to the right on the x-axis," said Leon. "Then we take the second number and move that many units up on the y-axis."

"Where the lines intersect is a point," Manuel added, pointing to the map. "Grace was at point $(1,2)$ when she saw your dog."

"Can you use the coordinate grid to find my puppy?" asked Ana. "She can be the treasure that we have to find."

"Let's give it a try," answered Leon.

Within minutes, everyone was in place. Ana waved to them all and slowly made her way to the little puppy. "Come here, puppy. Look at the nice treat I have for you!" she called, pulling a small dog bone from her pocket.

The puppy gave a happy bark and ran to Ana. It lay down at her feet and began munching on the bone. Quickly Ana buckled the collar snugly on her pet.

Manuel, Grace, and Leon ran up. "Hooray! We found the treasure," cheered Grace.

"Which way is she going?" Manuel radioed back.

"She's coming your way," answered Leon. "I see her in the distance. It looks as if she is at point (6,6)."

Manuel studied the map and smiled. "Ana, we are close to finding the treasure!"

He clicked the button on the walkie-talkie. "I think our hunt is just about over, everyone. Go to these points so we can corner the treasure. Grace, move one unit to the right and one unit down. Leon, slowly move up behind the treasure to get to point (6,6). I'm going to point (5,7), and Ana will move straight down three units."

"This plan should work," agreed Grace. "I'm on my way."

"I still see the puppy," said Leon. "She won't get past me!"

Read·Think·Write What are the four points where the friends will be positioned?

Grace traced a horizontal line segment up two units and plotted a point at (4,7). "I will walk a straight line to this point," she said. "I'll stay at that spot and catch our treasure if she tries to run toward the playground."

"Ana and I will go up toward the lake," Manuel said. He plotted a point at (6,10) on the map. "The lake is the boundary of the park. The puppy can't go any farther, so we should be able to corner her."

Ana and Manuel were almost to the edge of the park when they heard the crackle of the walkie-talkie. It was Leon. "Grace was right. That puppy is fast! She was here near the tables, but she scampered away just as I was about to catch her."

The friends raced past the ball field and headed toward a large rock. When they got there, they found Grace gasping for breath. "Your little puppy is fast," she panted. "I just couldn't keep up with her."

"At least you saw her," said Leon. "Now, we need to spread out." He took a pencil out of his pocket and drew a horizontal line segment on the map. It was a straight line two units to the right of the rock. Then he placed a dot on the intersection. "I'll go look for the treasure at this point."

Read·Think·Write Which point will Leon go to on the map?

"Wait a minute," said Leon. "That's it—treasure. You should call your puppy Treasure!"

"That's a perfect name," agreed Ana. "She certainly is a treasure to me!"

Manuel added, "And don't forget, she is a golden retriever!"

Ana laughed. "I never could have found my puppy without your help. So, to thank you, let's go to point (1,4) and I'll buy all of us a treat!"

"You're an expert with ordered pairs and a graph now," said Leon. "How would you like to join our next treasure hunt?"

"I'd love it!" exclaimed Ana. "But next time, you bring the treasure!"

Read·Think·Write Where are the friends going to get a treat?

11

1. What is an ordered pair?

2. Look at the graph. What is the ordered pair of the plotted point?

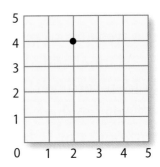

3. Find the point (5,1) on the graph.

4. Visualize Think about the ordered pair (3,5). What point would you plot if you moved two units right and one unit down?

Activity

Work with a partner. Use a sheet of graph paper to draw a map of the classroom. Draw a coordinate grid over the top of the map. Then take turns hiding an object without your partner watching. Tell your partner the coordinates where the object can be found. Now your partner can use the map to locate the hidden object.